Measures of Home

Measures of Home

poems by

Leela Gandhi

RAVI DAYAL Publisher
Delhi

Published by
RAVI DAYAL Publisher
51 E Sujan Singh Park
New Delhi 110003

Distributed by
ORIENT LONGMAN LTD
Bangalore Bhubaneshwar Calcutta Chennai
Ernakulam Guwahati Hyderabad Jaipur
Lucknow Mumbai New Delhi Patna

ISBN 81 7530 023 X

Typeset by Rastrixi, New Delhi 110070
Printed at Pauls Press, New Delhi 110020

For
Bronte Adams

Acknowledgments

This slim volume has been a long time in the making, and its coming to life has been overseen by many friends and well-wishers. I wish to thank Ramin Gray, my first reader; Suman Gupta, Tarun Saint, Nirmalya Samanta and P.K. Vijayan for their conversation, criticism and poetic companionship; Pauline Nestor for her patient encouragement and advice; Andrea Goldsmith for her painstaking reading and response to this manuscript; Indu and Ramu Gandhi and Veenapani Chawla, who, miraculously, remain encouraging about every project; and Ravi Dayal, whose astute and careful editorial suggestions were instrumental in the realisation of this manuscript. Finally, it is to Ruth Vanita that I owe the greatest thanks, for teaching me how to write, and for sharing with me the skill and inspiration that informs both her prose and her poetry.

Contents

Invocation

These songs of Summertown
Rise from the ground:
Hail rain, hold sun,
Let my vowels resonate
My verbs resound
Until the singing's done,
My songs sung.

Content

In origins, exigencies, musings, easings,
Four measures of biography.

The snug sobriety of home and history,
Smug gestures of protest and prodigality,
And having flown too far, anxiety.
The counterpoint of verse, maturity,
Until the first grey hair,
Separating charm from eccentricity,
Teases the past with propriety.

The Gift (I)

Your scriptures of secrecy
forbade defeating stories,
the bitter world's indemnity.

What sum for negligence? No price
repairs a lifetime's resignation.
I saw the rigour in your eyes

Brave, impassive, secreting their history,
refusing dull lamentations
from my guilty éscritoire.

You need daughters, grandchildren, to endure
the greedy world, happy lives, released,
the truth is still, with me, secure.

I'll write forgiveness, instead,
always of the best,
leaving the worst unspoken, unsaid.

The Gift (II)

1

A long time ago, when my father, a magician,
Taught me to whistle the 'Ode to Joy',
Notes succeeding notes, and heads held high,
My toddler smile, drawing breath,
Exorcised the air, tuning the words I spoke,
And those he spared.

Now I a lesser Ulysses behold:
Just a little man, growing old.

2

With age my father's face takes on the cast of grief.
His features, tragic in repose, achieve
The old mask — Lear's? — as though some jester
Turned adversary, inverts a smile,
And with it goes the world's sobriety.

Nothing savage here, just flesh, newly torn
With thinking, the loss — the death? — of daughters.

Snapshot

The family photograph
Hangs askew around my neck
It is heavy and it bites.

It must have been a hot day
When we set off, to smile
And snap into the lens.

We are nestled both
In the crook of his arm.
The genetic precedence of his teeth
Is gnashed in mine.
She demurs,
Smiling through her eyes.

Elsewhere in the house
Pictures of Arcadia
Recollect the past.

Genealogy

My broken family tree
Desiccates the wind.
Ringed, rimmed, and solitary,
Bequeaths its pain to me,
That I may rescind, resolve,
The fractured past,
Forgive the things unsaid,
The hands unclasped.

Of Holy Matrimony

Socratic *dulcedo*:
The philosopher honeys the hemlock
That he drinks.
And now this:
An old man spitting ink.

Receiving, she ages.
Good woman
For all that may befall
Suffer and bear.
Too late to shoulder grief
She looks the other way.

Once around the flames
Seven circles of burning
Turn to wax.
And now this:
A house, a tenement
Ringing their eyes with rain.

Sometimes a daughter,
Prodigal and strange,
Returns to rob their history.

Grandmother

Blank eyes absorb the sky, a strand
Of hair defies, both wind and pain,
Her voice rising, breaks, upon a lullaby.
My grandmother, growing old, deciphers,
Daughters are verbs and sons ciphers.

Ashram: With Family

Once from Adyar, with amma's steel efficiency,
a pilgrimage portends wakefulness.
We're on the road before dawn concedes
to flutter in the sky. She's alert to the business
of travel: vats of thayyar saadam packed to please
highway hunger; her green cupboards gradually release
small sums. Our hectic soirée leaves me sick
for sleep, morose with adolescent humour.
It will take more than a grandmother from these parts
to make clever conversation at this hour.
Ma, unusually buoyant before noon, celebrates the car:
'Really amma, *so* much better than a bus' —
a white ambassador, dodging other
trucks with histrionic verve. I fuss,
inwardly, about God and families.
That was years ago.
There were no revelations that summer.

Ashram: Protest

'The governor is coming!'
A man in khaki shorts officiates the crowd,
rearranging worshippers in thick clusters of sobriety,
as though we were flowers — of some lesser sort.
A bouquet of women elaborates the conceit,
a child is propped against the wall,
its sleepy head denied retrocession.
The picture completed, attenuates
the scene, with uniform obeisance.

Let the pious laugh, untidily
under the ashoka tree,
happier to be free in prayer
than solid with religion.

A Catalogue for Prayer

For prayer, a room accustomed
To the shape of need, a sense of ease.
An honest room, well worn, well thumbed,
Where love has been allowed to please
Small beginnings, still conclusions of despair,
Your footfall agitating the supple air,
Home, conversations with my family,
Images, pictures, moved across the sea,
A night of dreams, the habit of God
In a day's routine.

Foreign Diary

Epilogue

Relative not coming to Australia,
Next of kin, first of kind, mother,
Left behind, like a house, a job,
Collateral, my evidence of darker ties,
To be informed, if I break my neck
In Wagga Wagga.

Friday

Long words in repose,
self-consciously still,
parrot the weather
in a long coat and sneakers

And so I stand (hugely clad)
at bus stops, shunning street lights,
pockets filled with breakfast,
and an apple, newly bought.

Saturday

Should we carry on like this,
ghost-writing before lunch?
Or gracefully surrender the day
to chips and hot chocolate on the lawns?

Sunday

Writing by candle-light
burning finger and thumb,
it's better to snuff it out.

Monday

Waking with the clouds
wasn't much fun either.
Clapham conversation and sugarless tea
spoke volumes.

Speak to me before day destructs
between now and duvet covers.

Tuesday

Today sick:
the virus flutters
the nights are long
my breath too short
to survive
the end of winter
the holdings
of your hand.

Wednesday

Arias bring unease,
I hanker after older etymologies.

The Looking Glass

1

'Look at me' — that's how it ends,
An imperative, not an invitation,
When the will breaks and the spirit bends.

Look at me — you did before
Love turned vigilante,
closing shop, shutting doors.

Prophesy my worth, through myopic eyes, today
Look at me — before you leave,
Without looking away.

2

When troubled, I search my face for flaws,
Seeking imperfections I might ablate, erase
And so refute, the shadows left by dreams,
Release the day to come, with cotton balls,
Subdue achings, breakings, and other warts,
Invite my nails to disrepair, make whole again.

3

Your letter comes
A mirror showing blemishes
A blue shard aloft, whose descent
Sharply, shatters, returns the face
You loved in vain.

4

There's more mystery to being loved than loving.
Why should you pick my face among a crowd
Of supplicants, counter my loneliness,
Forget my negligence, and loving, choose
To fill your days with thirst and pain?

5

I used to think of pain as the place
Where poems begun, refuse to end,
An excess of words, surfeit of artistry.
But more than these, it's a lack of capacity,
Penalty for the gluttony of love and hope,
The knowledge that everything can't be had
At once, and swallowing, sickens.
The lover and the friend, this world and that,
Divided, breaking open to show
The old eviscerate of blood and bones.

6

From time to time we choose someone and call them 'home'.
This is the fault which fissures our intent:
A subterranean vapidity, prefigured in the earth,
Whose floods and volcanoes, heat and cool our loves,
Bringing bridges down, breaking hearts.

7

When the vacant heart offers its tenancy,
Only the very rich, the very brave apply.
Hard lodging in these mirrored corridors,
No shadows, lies, no comfort here,
An unforgiving light becomes our arbiter.
Few have the means, the nerve to know,
This is all there was to love: cold feet
And the anxious angularities of desire.

8

In love, the looking glass is our nemesis,
Some hack, lover, god, surgeon in a crowd,
Smiles approvingly, looks proud —
For such eyes, hands, we needle up our pores,
Cement our cavities. Only the heart remains,
Waiting for a knife to turn.

That Incubus Love

1

I cannot remove pain from our reckonings
Or censor the pleasure that greetings gain.
I'm creatured by necessity, submit to chance,
Whatever love will bring.

But should you break, I'll follow
Piece upon piece, tooth for tooth released.
Call it weakness, faith, I shudder awake,
Drawing dull requiems from your eyes.

Why pleasure pain, its shattered frontier
Renders obsolete, fire and air,
And in the flames, gods made of nothing?

2

There is a demon inside me
Rankles with anger.
Its recrement upon my tongue
Fouls with lack of sleep.

Bruising my cuticles
It fills my eyes with terracotta rage
Punishing self with hate
Soul with emptiness.

Who will protect my love
From its head-battering falsettos,
Recondite my breath
And save me from extremity?

3

You want to unwrap me like a candle,
Only fire burns enough to bring
A candle down. I will melt, congeal,
Viscous and unclean, a liquid mess of fears,
A threadbare splutter in the dark,
A moment's ease, quite, quite fatigued,
Icarus to your heat, your gift turned ashen,
Your hands askew with grease.

Sex

Our desire wanting, we tried our love
And found it good enough without
This sex thing, this hip and lip thing.
Let other lovers sweat and grind,
Our love's refined, raising virtues from necessity.

More than these hands, eyes, fingertips,
Your voice, taxing the telephone,
Equips my shabby days with grace,
And brings me home to certainties —
Food, drink, conversation, this place.

Yet, in the night's grim abrasions,
This body suffers sense, and taking sleep for death,
Begs awakening, contests evasions,
Turns craven — no better than the rest,
No worse, drawing blood, drawing breath.

Mea Culpa

1

I too my bard obeying, pursue the test:
One, lessoned by my love, allows my arms to rest,
Embrace the other, who sings and they think best.
Sounding the flesh, I voice my penance next.

2

Sin of self-love repeating,
Your love accede, purveying
Virtue and pain, distorting
Pleasure with protestation.

It takes two to clasp a hand,
Two holdings to caress it,
To crush the bones, two hands
Enclose the fire made.

I have lit it too, darkly,
Concealed the flames unmade.
Desire, not arrogance, persisting,
Burnt the night away.

Recovery

There was once another
Left me to my Odyssey.

My return postponed
He expedites the loom.
No woman, he wearies of desire
And the licit puckerings of love,
Requites my passing on the telephone.

And love would yield its requiems
But that in malediction he kept me warm.

Homecoming

A bareness maligns our meetings, this time
Your eyes are parched and dry, your hands contrite,
Without respite, caress the air, neither touching
Nor pleasing. Our fractured interim delivers
New indemnities. Your stock is high, my price decreases.

Home

You have that gift of home, the power of nostalgia,
My stories cling to you, become your own
To share with strangers on foreign nights alone,
The comfort of memory. Your hemisphere
Completes the fractured circle of my history,
The omissions of departure, remakes, in gum trees.

In Flight

Inching across the sky, arrest my airborne mind:
This journey takes me hence, leaves you behind,
Until my thoughts return, to you inclined.
Some muse has kept us still, insured my rhyme
Against the words, gestures, and clauses,
Upon which songs subside, love pauses.

Quest

I'm troubled now by these kingfisher moments
Flashing through the air, grabbing bits of love,
Flecks of breath, the tired static of the phone,
The postman's mediations, the fat extremes
Of amnesia and insanity, the dissonance
Of summer clocks, foreshortening my return.

Retreat/Pastoral

I came here seeking expiation
found better comfort in these
still small hours

meditatively to heal
the year's rough traffic
my sleep alarming dreams

escape to wake with peace
watch the rain appease
the trees, and the terrors of agency

on the cool stone floors
a patch of green, the sea,
forfend sociability

it's good to be alone
with welcome silences,
it would be better still
if you were here with me.

Dreaming (I)

Night's here, days done.
Bits of dream anthologise
Hopelessly in my mind.
Will this corpus relieve
Dull hours of absence,
Subdue the seas,
And lead me through
Our covenant, to you?

Distance is inimical to truth,
Fanatical to pain

Are you dreaming too?
Somewhere in your cracked brown land,
Are you making plans to meet me, halfway,
Between desire and domesticity,
Between truth and pain?

lamplight, dusk:
we sit in equipoise
waiting for the guests
to arrive.

Dreaming (II)

Unrest is that slim moment between sleep and waking
When the body, seeking sense, craves the routine motions
Of water and air, but the mind, still dreaming of a world gone bad,
Shatters the morning with memory.

Dream

Last night, with the recklessness of sleep,
I dream your eviction from my room.
You are, of course, my mother —
what a cliché — and I, petulant, unlovely,
measure my freedom in empty rooms.

In the dream you quarrel,
with my mother's recalcitrance.
In the morning you smile,
with my mother's resignation.

I think I love you.
I think I'm sick for home.

Summer Pastiche

On days like these anxiety patchworks the horizon,
a tepid sky, well-worn, defies eternity.

The sun, too hot for growing things, makes hope recede,
the sea denies my feet, on the dry shore.

Suppose you change, one day, like this season,
turned cruel for variety, and look away?

Should I take the pain as fair exchange
for better weather, or wait, patiently, for the rain?

Love and Death

We quarrel bitterly, with the ache
of real quarrelling. I say, 'let me die' — with my
penchant for melodrama. You take
mortality more seriously, and start to cry.
I quicken to remorse, my words undo,
I meant to say, 'Be kind, don't make
me live alone and without you'.

Conversion

I remember a chill winter verandah, dead trees
And atmosphere; you were eloquent with honesty,
Wearing the brave face of love against the odds.
We spoke, circuitously, about some poem on female integrity:
'Women tell the truth, men secure lifetimes in duplicity.'
I think I acquiesced, I think there was some sophistry.

Matrimony

Of all the others you remain tempting
with civility. Grave, gentle, sane,
your courtesy exceeds the best,
confounds protest, requests invasion.

Should I accept, submit, agree, your prayers
concede, your lips admit, your hands permit,
our vows proceed.

Or leaving the circle of your gravity
adrift, persist. Alone, intact, and free?

Panegyric

1

Carrot cake, carrot cake
I have it all, I have it all:
A cheese, a roast, aperitif
That you and yours have fed upon

And you have loved me very well

2

From candy floss to angel bake
All sweetenings I have entertained
The figures of your verse transform
From woman I become a cake

Your words in syrup suffocate

3

Fattened with similitudes,
You've iced my breath with saccharine,
To bite, to chew and masticate
To nibble and negate the plate

That I am served upon

4

Of gristle and bone:
I am inedible, undrinkable,
A rind of lemon in my eyes
Puckers the mouth that sucks it

There is a famine where I stand.

To My Recalcitrant Muse

Two meanings of refrain have come to mind:
My will to sing, enforce my tongue to rhyme,
And still my muse, forbidding flight, remains unkind.

I must have killed her with verbosity,
In some prosaic gesture, spent my worth,
The words she had reserved for me.

Until restored to sound, I practice borrowed notes,
Others pace the stage, I watch aside,
Understudy saints, poets, fuller throats.

Vac

The poets insist it is true
Poems survive our afternoons,
Songs resurrect events
And elegies revive the dead.

If I made you into a word
Would you last longer that these lunches do?
Could I conjure your company with a breath,
With chanting, commit you to memory?

And when my youth, unseasoned, passes,
My hands fissure with care,
Will this verse, alone, sustain the flesh,
Restore me to your epithets?

Words, brazen, are very often false,
Changing things known into those imagined.
Sing as I may, you are gone, a day ago
And I am older by an equinox.

Katha

This story has been told before:
A poet admits two others to his prose,
Both struggling for priority,
One loves him, the other he desires.

Words of habit elegize
Old times and lullabies
Compete with newer sounds
Groping for signifiers.

He falters between the lines,
Framing his refrain:
Desiring, he will complain,
Where he is loved, retire.

Poems and poets both, practice promiscuity,
There is no fidelity in either men or words.

Valmiki: Shoka

Pain is the hunter's epiphany,
An arrow's preamble through
The listless forest air.

After the first excuse
Of flesh and feathers, a cry is heard,
After death, a clutch of words.

Pain is the hunter's quiver,
Each weapon, a sharpened quill,
Hurting the world into poetry.

Sur: Surdas

Otherwise a handicap, poetry hangs on a limb
Severed by the world's misgivings.
It takes a beggar's insouciance to spin
A song, to give a life away.
Poetry attempts the air on crutches, inchoate
And accidental, gives pause, takes pain,
Lives, on the sharp edges of absence,
In the rough silence of speaking things
Stammers its dissent, complains,
Makes whole again, compensates;
Where a foot should fall, lines endorse the earth,
A steady rhythm reforms the hunchback.
It takes a blind poet, scrabbling in the dark,
To letter the night with words, insight.

Homage to Emily Dickinson, After Pain

Our formal feeling when it comes, comes belatedly,
Like a chill on a good night, a season's afterthought,
The end of history, savage, contumely, overwrought
With pain, the flat refrain of casual years, casually
defeated.

Until, too late for these tight-lipped arrears,
The language of equity, hard-fisted, appears,
Polite, policing, juridical, ill at ease,
A harsh civility of anxious words, anxiously
repeated.

This is the cost of sorrow, the price of dignity; our testimony,
Speaking as strangers should in hostile company,
Stammers its excuse, attempts amnesia,
In the place of love, a quarantine, hopelessly
conceited.

On Reading You Reading Elizabeth Bishop

You lend me Bishop to improve my mind,
Trusting yours, I turn the pages, find,
This poet is your confidant and friend,
While I, consigned to where her margins end,
Must annotate your litany, with apologies:
It wasn't me, I wasn't mean, I didn't mean,
To stammer in mid-flight; the weather intervened,
A dark brown land turned green, I was across the sea,
I tried, I couldn't make it over Brooklyn bridge.
Sweet plaintiff, I am powerless against the
Influence you wield, cannot sing in self-defence.
Why use the poets for advocacy?
Let us quarrel in our own words, edge to edge,
Choosing conversation over bibliography.

On Vermeer: Female Interiors

You could take these pictures as the same
Old theme: happy women, happily, shelling peas
(reading, writing — same difference), inane,
Before evening brings the sweaty masonry
Home, on heavy knees: thick male shapes, thickening
The air with petulance, slamming windows, appeal,
Demanding drink until the women, sickening,
Look up, breaking their reverie, the colours congeal.
Except, Vermeer didn't do evening scenes this way,
the chiaroscuro intervenes, taking light for play,
Leaving officers, husbands in the dark, unseen.
Alone, untaught, these women are pristine,
The corpus preserves interiors; a bright continuum
Of female heads, conspiring to still life, live on.

At the Emporia, Baba Kharak Singh Marg

In a smart shop for travellers going home
My friend watches the carnelian
With sad cat eyes, cautious and alone
She holds the orange stone in quiet colloquium.

Around her, shoppers, shuffling their desires,
Animate the morning, compete with other buyers,
Mirrors catch quick rehearsals of return,
The doors revolve, her thoughts confirm

Sadness: buying is going away, taking leaving,
A mess of memorabilia for a year's escape;
The traveller's conceit gathers a grieving
World into a suitcase, a film to break

Monotony informs, there are places otherwise
Than the wet suburb in Bogna Regis,
Where tea is brewed *in extremis*
And you grow old, your stories are untold; what price

Will stop the daily drone, pious, repeating,
Newspaper, weather, neighbours, and the phone
Ringing in the mind's unease; a life on hold defeating.
What's a necklace to this destiny, what's in a stone?

Troubled by her counterpoint, the salesman intervenes:
'Would madam like some pearls, I can show . . . '
But she is still, unmoved, her eyes appeal,
She doesn't want to shop, she doesn't want to go.

Memory

1

In Radcliffe square, unharmed by the wind,
we swap histories. Ramin, delighting
in my former fatness, like a child,
wants detail and repetition:
'How fat', 'How small',
'Tell me again'. As though in telling,
time would stop, space dissolve, and
the grey stones become a gopuram
in Iran, a pub in Chattisgarh.

2

I have learnt since to think of history with suspicion,
as the place where love atrophies, stories are untold.
I have learnt that stories lie.

3

But perhaps he was right after all,
as children often are, to memorise the fabulous,
to hold me like a piece of glass against the light:
a bauble made precious,
a babble brought to verse,
a love completed.